W9-CIF-362

DISGUSTING & DREADFUL SCIENCE

Glaring Light

and other eye-burning rays

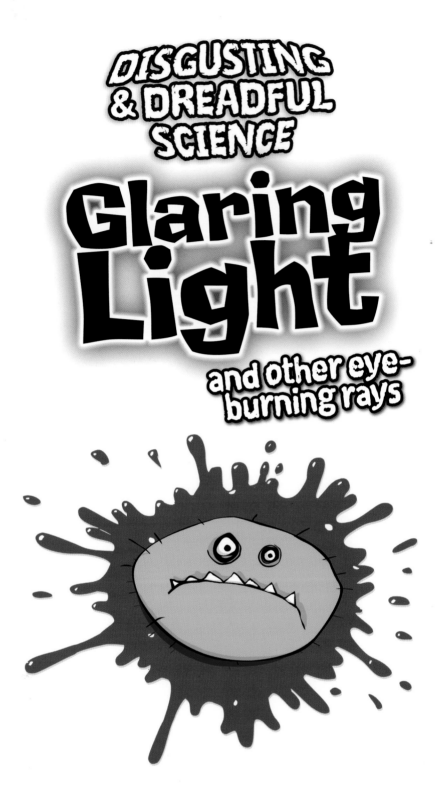

by Anna Claybourne

Crabtree Publishing Company
www.crabtreebooks.com

Crabtree Publishing Company
www.crabtreebooks.com
1-800-387-7650

Published in Canada
Crabtree Publishing
616 Welland Avenue
St. Catharines, ON
L2M 5V6

Published in the USA
Crabtree Publishing
PMB 59051
350 Fifth Ave, 59th Floor
New York, NY 10118

Printed in Hong Kong/092012/BK20120629

Author: Anna Claybourne
Editorial director: Kathy Middleton
Editors: Nicola Edwards, Adrianna Morganelli
Proofreader: Crystal Sikkens
Designer: Elaine Wilkinson
Picture Researcher: Clive Gifford
**Production coordinator and
   Prepress technician:** Ken Wright
Print coordinator: Katherine Berti

Published by Crabtree Publishing in 2013

First published in 2013 by Franklin Watts
Copyright © Franklin Watts 2013

Picture acknowledgements:
Corbis images: 14t (Leah Warkentin/Design Pics); 19c (© Minnesota Historical Society). **fotolia:** 17cl (theogott). iStockphoto.com: title page (Dean Murray), eyeball cartoon (Elaine Barker); 7t (snipes213); 10tr (juniorbeep); 13t (Lezh); 13r (Gewoldi); 16c (pzAxe); 17b (Zitramon); 20cr and cover (mbortolino); 20bl (hakusan); 21tr (Henrik5000); 26bl (tap10); 27t (Jodi Jacobson); 27c (PlainView); 27b (craftvision). NASA: 5c; 9b. **Nature Picture Library:** 15b (Wild Wonders of Europe/Hodalic). Ryan Hagerty, **US Fish and Wildlife Service:** 13c. Science Photo Library: 12t (Jacopin); 24tl (Wim Van Egmond/Visuals Unlimited, Inc); 28b (Eye of Science). **Shutterstock.com:** angry monster cartoon (Yayayoyo); cover main image (Olly); 4tr (matt); 4tl (Memo Angeles); 4bl (Wichan Konchan); 5br (Zholobrov Vadim); 6t (Olga Popova); 6b (Valeriy Lebedev); 7c (Luca Flor); 8b (MarchCattle); 9t (perensanz); 10cl (copperman); 10c (Architecte®); 11tr (Julia Mihatsch); 11cl (Quayside); 11bl (Trent Townsend); 11br (Panachai Cherdchucheep); 12c (billyhoiler); 12b (Anneka); 15t (Andreas Koeberl); 15c (Simonalvinge); 17t (Augusto Cabral); 18t (Lasse Kristensen); 18b and back cover (Chianuri); 19t (Shane Gross); 20t (advent); 22t (yxowert); 22cl (Alex Kalmbach); 23tl (Anteromite); 23ctl (Katarzyna Mazurowska); 23tr (Geoffrey Jones); 23cr (Arnoud Quanjer); 23cb (Vadim Kozlovsky); 24cr (Cathy Keifer); 24b and back cover (Julia Mihatsch); 25t (Riegsecker); 25c (David Carillet); 26t (Javier Brosch); 28tl (Petr Bukal); 28tr (Dmitry Kalinovsky); 29tl (Sergej Khakimullin); 29tr (Fox Pictures); 29b and cover (DM7). **Visuals Unlimited**: (JimVan Egmond): 24tl. **Wikipedia:** 16tr; 17cr and 26cr (Sir Godfrey Kneller); 21c (Samir).

All other illustrations by Graham Rich

Every attempt has been made to clear copyright. Should there be any inadvertent omission, please apply to the publisher for rectification.

**Library and Archives Canada
Cataloguing in Publication**

Claybourne, Anna
     Glaring light and other eye-burning rays / Anna Claybourne.

(Disgusting and dreadful science)
Includes index.
Issued also in electronic format.
ISBN 978-0-7787-0945-9 (bound).--ISBN 978-0-7787-0955-8 (pbk.)

     1. Light--Juvenile literature. I. Title. II. Series: Disgusting and dreadful science

QC360.C53 2013   j535   C2012-907289-3

**Library of Congress
Cataloging-in-Publication Data**

CIP available at Library of Congress

Contents

Flash!

Ow! My eyes! A bright light can give you a fright—like when a camera flashes at you, or someone switches on your light on a dark winter morning. Light can also hurt you. It can damage your eyes and your skin. We are very sensitive to bright light, yet there are some types of light we can't see at all!

Light and sight

Too much light can be a pain, but most of the time, it's very useful. There's light all around us, shining from the Sun, the stars, streetlights, and other light sources. It bounces off most other objects, too. So we can detect all kinds of things around us by sensing light with our eyes. From the tip of your own nose, to the screen on your phone, to a star billions of kilometers away—as long as light is coming from them somehow (and your eyes are working) you can see them all.

Argh! Bright light!

What IS light?

You know light when you see it... but what is it actually made of? Light is a form of energy that shines out from burning or glowing objects. We don't see it moving as it goes so fast, but it travels along in the form of tiny energy waves called light rays. This picture shows how they move.

Light forms

Light isn't just the bright rays that we can see. It comes in many forms and has some amazing qualities. X-rays, radio waves, and microwaves are all types of light. In its different forms, light can cut through metal, zap zits, make hidden bloodstains glow, sizzle your skin, and slice into your eyeballs! It zooms faster than a speeding bullet (about 300,000 times faster!) and even lets us look back in time...

See for Yourself

Light sources

Our main light source is our nearest star, the Sun. It gives out light because it's made of fiery, exploding gases. However, there are many other light sources, both natural and artificial. How many can you think of? (A look through this book might help!)

Earth from space, showing artifical lights (orange), sunlight (white), and the Northern Lights (green)

Wearing sunglasses and wide-brimmed hats in bright sunlight is not just about glamour—it's also good sense! They protect your eyes and skin from harmful rays.

Ouch!

Bright light is painful because your eyes contain special light-detecting cells. They have to be very sensitive so that you can see in dim light. Very strong light can overload and damage them. If this happens, your eye sends pain signals to your brain to make you shut your eyes as soon as possible.

Stre-e-etch yourself!

When you look at yourself in a spoon, a funhouse mirror, or through water, you look all stretched, squashed, or wonky. The same thing can happen to people's eyes when they wear thick glasses.

Lines of light

Rays of light normally travel in straight lines to our eyes. If there's nothing in the way, everything looks normal. But light can sometimes bend or change direction.

Refraction

Refraction happens when light passes out of one see-through substance, such as air, water, or glass, into another. This makes the light rays change direction slightly.

That's why a straight straw can look broken when it stands in a glass of water, and your legs can look strangely short when you are standing in a swimming pool.

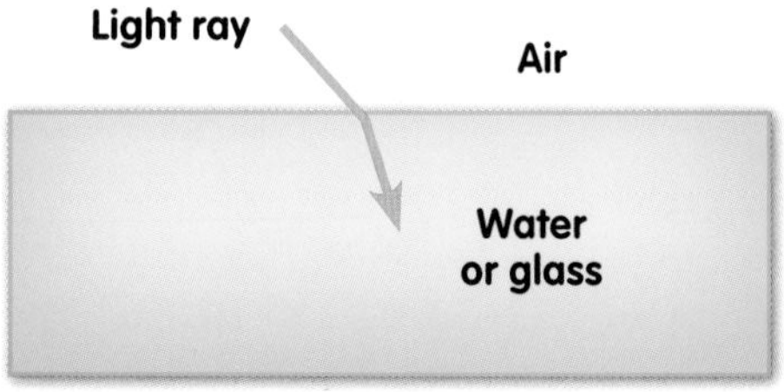

Light ray

Air

Water or glass

A curved piece of glass, like a magnifying glass lens, bends the light in different directions, making things look stretched and super-sized.

Reflection

Reflection happens when light bounces off a shiny surface like a mirror. If the mirror is flat, the light rays stay in the same pattern.

If the mirror is curved or bumpy, the light rays shoot off in different directions so you see a stretched or squashed image, like the one in this bus mirror.

Light rays   **Reflection**

Mirror

DID YOU KNOW?

If you're ever lost in the wild, you can use something shiny (like a mirror, CD, or tin foil) to reflect sunlight and signal to passing planes for help.

Stretchy shadows

As light travels in straight lines, it can't usually curve around objects. Instead, an object that isn't see-through casts a shadow, or a dark area where the light rays are blocked. You can make giant shadows when the Sun is low in the sky, like the cowboy in the picture above.

See for Yourself

Casting shadows

When an object is very close to a light source, it casts a bigger shadow. Try cutting a spooky shape out of cardboard (or use your hand) and hold it near a lamp or flashlight in a dark room. Can you cast funny shadows on the wall?

7

Time travel

Light takes time to travel across space. That means it can show us things from the past—depending on how far away it started its journey. Confused? Here's how it works.

Yikes!

If the Sun suddenly went out, we would only find out eight minutes later. But don't worry, scientists think the Sun will be around for at least another five billion years.

The speed of light

Light travels VERY fast. Its normal speed is around 621,371,192 miles per hour or one billion (1,000,000,000 km/h). When you flick on your bedroom lamp, light zooms from the bulb around the room so fast, it seems instant. But in space, distances are much greater. For example, the Sun is about 93 million miles (150 million km) away from Earth. So light from the Sun, whizzing through space at over 600 million mph (965,606,400 km/h), takes about eight minutes to reach us.

Look back in time...

Most things in space are even farther away than the Sun. There are stars and galaxies that are so far away, the light from them takes millions of years to reach us. And that means that we see them not now, but in the past—as they were millions of years ago. **WEIRD!**

Light travels a million times faster than a jumbo jet!

Light years

A **light year** is a measure of distance. It's the distance that light travels in a year. Since light goes so fast, that's a long way—about 6 trillion miles (10 trillion km).

OUR SUN

Our Sun is

93 million miles (50 million km)

from Earth. It takes light

8 minutes

to reach us.

We see it as it was 8 minutes ago.

A STAR

If a star is

6 trillion miles (10 trillion km)

from Earth, it takes light

1 light year

to reach us.

We see it as it was a year ago.

See for Yourself

Yourself in the past

Even looking at yourself in a mirror means you're seeing yourself in the (very recent!) past, because of the time light takes to travel to the mirror, then back to your eyes. If you set up two mirrors facing each other, you can see a lot of reflections of yourself, stretching away into the distance. Each one shows a slightly younger version of you, until they disappear.

A DISTANT STAR

If a star is

100 light years

from Earth, it takes light

100 years

to reach us.

We see it as it was 100 years ago.

AND SO ON...

A snapshot in time

Using powerful telescopes, we can now look back into the history of the Universe. This picture, taken by NASA's Hubble Space Telescope in 2000, shows a star as it looked several thousand years ago, surrounded by a cloud of gas.

Green slime

Dip a stick into a pond, and you're likely to pull out a trail of damp, dangly, dripping green slime. YUCK! But what is pond slime, and why is it green? For that matter, why are most plants green? It's all to do with light.

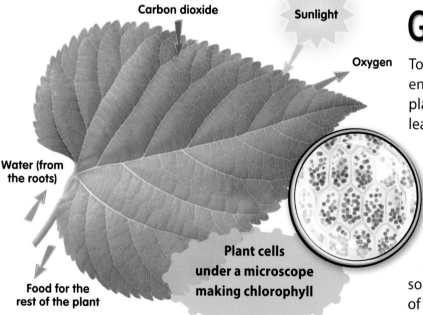

Carbon dioxide

Sunlight

Oxygen

Water (from the roots)

Food for the rest of the plant

Plant cells under a microscope making chlorophyll

Green energy

To live, plants need light. They use light energy from the Sun to build all their plant parts, such as their stems, roots, leaves, fruits, and seeds, using gases from the air and water from the ground. To do this, plants use a process called **photosynthesis** (meaning "making with light"). It happens inside the cells in a plant's leaves. They contain a bright green chemical called chlorophyll that can soak up sunlight and convert it to a kind of energy the plant can use.

 ## See for Yourself

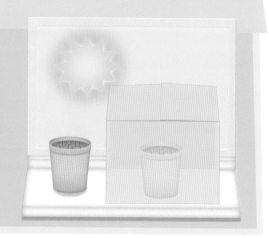

Darkness or light?

Fill two small pots with soil, and plant a couple of seeds in each. (Sunflower seeds or apple seeds are good). Stand one pot on a sunny windowsill, and the other next to it inside a closed cardboard box. Water both plants every day. How well do they grow with and without light?

Sun grabbers

To soak up as much light as they can, the green parts of a plant spread out to catch the Sun's rays. Trees spread out their leaves wide and high. Green waterweed spreads out across ponds. Pond slime is often a mixture of water-loving plants, such as waterweed, and **algae**. Algae is like a plant but has no roots or leaves and it sometimes spreads out across rivers and lakes to cover the whole water surface.

Great green food machine

If it weren't for plants, we'd all starve to death! Plants use light energy to make plant parts. All those leaves, fruits, and seeds provide food for plant-eating animals. Those animals get eaten by meat-eating animals. So whether you're a strict vegetarian or a burger-loving meat-muncher, you would have nothing to eat at all if it weren't for photosynthesis.

Come closer, little fly!

Yuck!

Some plants have ferocious appetites. They catch themselves extra snacks by trapping and gobbling up insects, or even frogs or mice! Pitcher plants (right) have pots with slippery slides. When animals slip in, they fall into the plant's digesting juices (like those in your tummy), which dissolve the creature so the plant can soak it up!

11

All about eyeballs

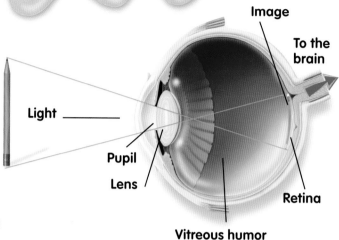

Image
To the brain
Light
Pupil
Lens
Retina
Vitreous humor

As we live on a sunlit planet, we're surrounded by light all day long. We have developed the ability to detect light, as a way of sensing our surroundings. Most animals have done the same. To collect light, we use a brilliant invention of nature —the round, squidgy eyeball.

DID YOU KNOW?

Some people find eyeballs very tasty, and eat them as a delicacy—especially fish and sheep eyes.
CHEWY!

How eyeballs work

Eyeballs are basically light-catchers. Light enters through the **pupil** at the front, and passes through a clear lens that bends the light rays. This casts a sharp, upside-down image onto the **retina**, a patch of light-detecting cells at the back of the eyeball. They turn the image into signals and send them to the brain, which flips it upright again.

Two eyes, 3-D vision

Why do we have two eyes? An obvious reason is so that we can still see if we lose one. Having two eyes also means we see each object from two slightly different angles. This lets our brain work out how far away things are, giving us 3-D vision. Human eyes can also distinguish about 10 million different shades of color.

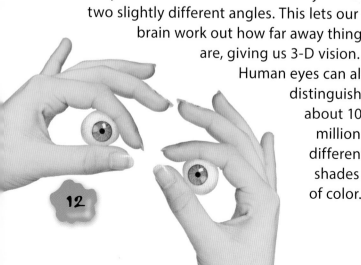

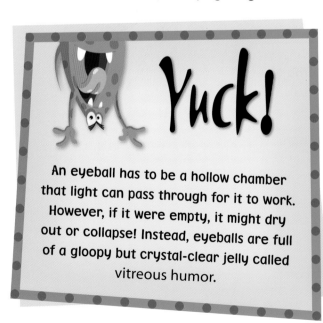

Yuck!

An eyeball has to be a hollow chamber that light can pass through for it to work. However, if it were empty, it might dry out or collapse! Instead, eyeballs are full of a gloopy but crystal-clear jelly called vitreous humor.

Eyes everywhere

Most animals have two eyes, but some have a lot more. Spiders have eight eyes. Have a look at this jumping spider (left) and see if you can spot them all!

Many insects have compound eyes, made up of hundreds or even thousands of light detectors, each with its own lens. You can see them in the big bulging eyes of the fly below.

Strange eyes

The animal world has come up with some crazy-looking eye designs.

• The barreleye fish has big eyeballs that point upward, inside its see-through head!

• A stalk-eye fly's eyes are on stalks that can be longer than its body.

• The colossal squid has the world's biggest eyeballs. They're the size of footballs!

• This caterpillar has fake eyes to scare off any creatures who may want to eat it.

Optical illusions

Our brains sometimes get confused by the signals coming from our eyeballs. Look at this optical illusion. Which of the two white circles is bigger?

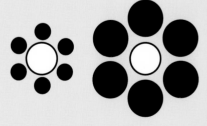

They're actually both the same size.

Dark and spooky!

It's nightime, it's dark, and you can hear a strange creaking noise —heeeelp! Are you scared of the dark? A lot of people are, even adults.

Turn the light on!

Darkness is what happens when there's no light around (or very little). Light has been important to humans since prehistoric times. We need it to see where we are and what's around us. In the dark, we feel nervous because it's harder to see any dangers nearby. Even if you know you're safe and sound in your own room, your brain can't help noticing spooky shapes in the shadows!

Life without light

Could we live without light? Besides the fact that we'd have no food (see page 11), we need sunlight. When it shines on our skin, our bodies make vitamin D, which helps us to fight off germs and keep our bones strong.

Ouch!

If you don't get enough vitamin D, you can get a horrible illness called rickets. It makes your bones painful, bendy, and weak, and your teeth sore.

Too much light!

Darkness can be a good thing, too. We sleep best when it's really dark. Streetlights, buildings, and vehicles can cause "light pollution", meaning that in some areas it's never really truly dark. This can annoy astronomers, as they need proper darkness to view the stars. Large telescopes (right) are often located in empty deserts or on high mountains, away from city lights.

A telescope in Hawaii

Creatures of the dark

Some animals prefer darkness. **Nocturnal** creatures, like moths and owls (above), usually hide during the daytime and come out at night. Some animals, known as troglobites, live in caves, where it's dark all the time. They are often blind and pale-skinned, like this strange-looking olm (below), which lives in underground rivers.

See for Yourself

Pupil play

Stand in front of a mirror in a dimly lit room. Then switch a light on and watch your eyes. Your pupils change size to take in less light when it's bright and more light when it's dark.

Seeing sense

Though we've always lived with light, it's taken us a long time to understand it. These brilliant scientists discovered all sorts of things about how light works.

Amazing Alhazen

Alhazen lived in Egypt around 1,000 years ago and did hundreds of experiments with light, refraction, reflection, eyes, and eyesight. He found that light travels in straight lines, and showed how it enters the eye. Until then, many people thought that eyes worked by sending out invisible rays that landed on objects. Alhazen saw that it was the other way around—light rays went from objects into the eye.

Amazing!

 ## See for Yourself

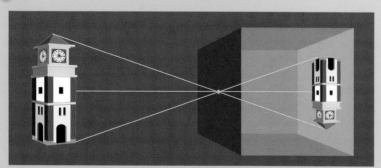

Alhazen's camera

Alhazen invented the camera obscura **(or "dark room"), which works like an eyeball. Light rays enter the room through a small hole or pinhole, and create an upside-down image on the wall inside.**

You can make your own camera obscura in a small room on a sunny day. Make the room as dark as possible. Tape cardboard or a thick cloth over the window to completely block out the light. Make a tiny hole in the cardboard or cloth. An upside-down view of the outside world should appear on the opposite wall.

How fast is that?!

In 1667, Galileo tried to measure how fast light was. He and his assistant stood on two hilltops in the dark, flashing lanterns at each other to see how long a signal took to pass between them. Galileo decided light must travel very fast—at least 10 times faster than sound. Other scientists attempted to measure it too, but it wasn't until 1862 that Leon Foucault finally pinned down the exact speed of light (page 8). He did it by using mirrors, math, and very clever measuring equipment.

DID YOU KNOW?

Foucault was going to be a doctor, but switched to physics because he was scared of blood!

Isaac's eyeballs

Around the year 1700, Isaac Newton, one of the greatest scientists ever, also studied light. He found that shining white light through a **prism,** a wedge-shaped piece of glass, could bend it and split it into different colors. (The same thing happens when sunlight shines through raindrops, making a rainbow.) Newton also studied eyeballs and invented a new type of telescope.

Newton experimented with his own eyeball by sticking a bodkin (blunt needle) behind it to see if it changed his eyesight. It did...

DON'T try this at home!

I put it between my eye and the bone...and pressing my eye with the end of it, there appeared several white, dark, and colored circles.

Microscopic monsters

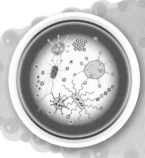

When microscopes were first invented, scientists were shocked to find tiny wriggling bacteria and creepy-crawlies living in water, soil, and even on people's teeth. UGH!

Making sparks

When it gets dark at home, you probably just flick on the electric light. Hundreds of years ago though, lights and lamps were a bit more basic.

Burning bright

You can make light by setting something on fire. Burning is a kind of chemical reaction. It makes substances break down and form other substances, and this gives off energy as heat and light. Of course, if you just set fire to a stick or a piece of paper, it will soon go out, and it could be dangerous. So a long time ago, people invented lamps and candles to burn fuel more slowly and safely.

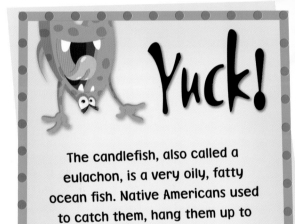

Yuck!

The candlefish, also called a eulachon, is a very oily, fatty ocean fish. Native Americans used to catch them, hang them up to dry, stick wicks in them, then use them as candles!

Wax and wicks

Candles can be made of many kinds of fat or wax, including beeswax or smelly whale or sheep fat. As a candle burns, the wax melts and soaks up into the stringy wick. The wax then turns into a gas or vapor in the air. The vapor burns, giving a steady light.

Hey! Leave my head alone!

Oil lamps

Simple oil lamps work in the same way as candles. They are filled with oil, which soaks into a wick, and the wick is lit at the other end. One popular kind of lamp oil came from the head of the sperm whale. People liked it because it wasn't as stinky as some other whale oils.

This photograph shows people in Minneapolis, U.S.A., gathered to see the first illumination of electric carbon arc lamps in 1883. But carbon lamps were very smoky and smelly, so light bulbs eventually took over (see page 20).

Early electricity

Candles and lamps with a flame were very risky. There were a lot of fires before electric lights took over. The first ever electric lamp glowed in 1809, more than 200 years ago. Scientist and inventor Humphry Davy linked a battery to a strip of carbon, making electricity flow through it. It heated up and glowed.

See for Yourself

Making sparks

Some materials give off a tiny bit of light when you break or tear them. Three examples are snapping or crushing a mint ; unrolling duct tape; or tearing open a self-adhesive envelope. Try these in complete darkness, such as under a blanket in a dark room, and you might see sparks! *

* Don't worry. These are not dangerous. They are just light sparks and won't set fire to your blanket!

Brilliant inventions

When you come up with an amazing idea—ding!—a light bulb appears above your head! (At least, it does if you're a cartoon.) The light bulb itself was a brilliant, simple idea. It changed our lives—just like many other great light-related inventions.

Who invented the light bulb?

Thomas Edison is famous for inventing the light bulb in the 1870s. Several inventors came up with their own versions, but Edison was the first to develop one that was easy to make, sell, and use.

In a traditional light bulb, electricity flows through a tightly coiled metal filament, making it glow. The **filament** is inside a pear-shaped glass case, filled with a gas that helps it last longer. Today, modern inventors have come up with new types of light bulbs, like the energy-saving one on the right.

The changing shape of light bulbs over the years

Lasers

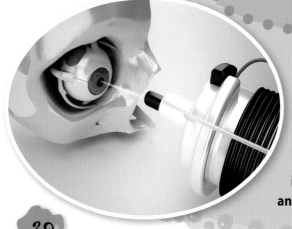

The laser, invented in 1960, is an intense, narrow beam of light that can be focused on a single point. Powerful, high-energy laser beams can cut through metal. They're also used to cut through body parts—for example in laser eye surgery, when a laser vaporizes part of your eyeball to reshape it. Gentler laser beams are used in CD players, light shows, barcode scanners, and to zap zits!

Cat's eyes

In 1933, Percy Shaw had a great idea when he saw a cat's eyes shining in the night as he drove along a clifftop road. His invention, the cat's eye, reflects a car's headlights so the driver can see the roadside and road markings—no batteries required! Today, there are millions of cat's eyes all over the world.

Yuck!

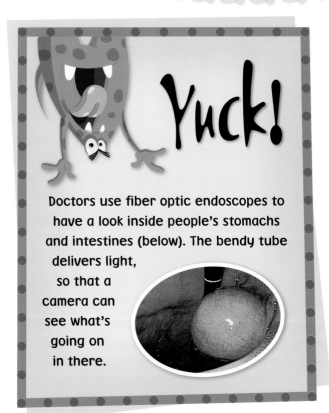

Doctors use fiber optic endoscopes to have a look inside people's stomachs and intestines (below). The bendy tube delivers light, so that a camera can see what's going on in there.

Optical fibers

Optical fibers are long, thin, bendy glass tubes. Light can travel along inside the tubes, bouncing off the inside walls, and shine out at the other end. This works even if the fibers twist, bend, or go around corners. So this brilliant invention is a great way to send light from one place to another, without it having to go in straight lines. Optical fibers date from the 1840s, but are used in a lot of modern inventions, like lamps and computer cables.

 # See for Yourself

Curving light

This experiment uses water to make a simple fiber optic tube. You need a clear plastic bottle with a small hole in the side (ask an adult to make the hole). Stand the bottle on the edge of a sink or bathtub, fill it with water, and shine a flashlight at the side opposite the hole. As water flows out of the hole, let it fall onto your hand. You should see a spot of light that has traveled through the curved water "tube."

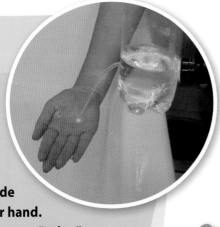

Spectrum-tacular!

We think of light as glowing and colorful—something we can see. In fact, visible light is just part of a huge range of different types of light energy—some of them frighteningly powerful. We can't see most of them, but we can detect them, and we use them for all sorts of things.

The light we can see, visible light, has medium-sized waves and is in the middle of the spectrum. Blue light has the shortest waves, ranging through the colors of the rainbow to red light, which has the longest.

The whole spectrum

The range of energy types is called the **electromagnetic spectrum**. You can see a diagram of it below.

Light energy travels in waves, and the different types have different wavelengths. That means the length of each wave, from the crest (top) of one to the crest of the next.

We use radio waves to carry signals long distances.

● ELF/VLF are sometimes used for signal broadcasting.

Extremely Low Frequency (ELF)

Very Low Frequency (VLF)

Radio waves (short waves)

Microwaves

Infrared radiation

Visible light

Ultraviolet radiation

X-rays

Gamma rays

At this end of the spectrum, the waves are very long.

At this end of the spectrum, the waves are very short, and carry a lot of energy.

Microwaves heat things up, so we use them in microwave ovens.

DID YOU KNOW?

Blood glows under ultraviolet light. At murder scenes, UV light is used to detect the faintest smears and fingerprints that might be left, even after the killer has tried to clean them up.

Hot things give off **infrared light**. We can detect them with special cameras.

Ultraviolet light is invisible to us, but some animals, like scorpions, glow when it shines on them! No one has yet found out why.

X-rays shine through many substances, and help us take pictures of our insides.

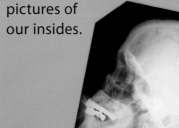

Gamma rays are powerful energy rays that come from some types of materials. They can kill germs but they can also cause severe sickness.

Signs like this warn you when there's a high risk from exposure to deadly radiation.

Yikes!

Being hit by gamma rays can cause vomiting and diarrhea, make your hair fall out, burn your skin, and that's just a small amount. A big dose can be deadly!

Glowing beasts

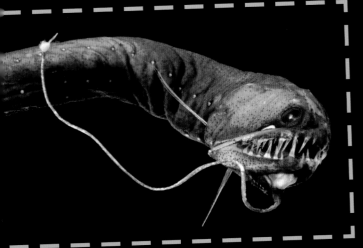

I magine having your own glowing lights built into your body! Some animals really do have this, thanks to bioluminescence (which means "living light"). They use their lights to help them see in the dark, send each other messages, lure prey, or help with camouflage.

Dragon in the depths

Deep down in the sea, sunlight can't reach through the water, so it's very dark. Sea creatures that live down here often have glowing lights on their bodies. The scaleless black dragonfish (above) is one. It has tiny spotlights on its body, and bigger lights on the ends of long tendrils. Scientists think these attract prey, which the dragonfish then snaps up.

Anyone want a date?

Brilliant bugs

Fireflies are creepy-crawlies with bright glowing tails. They're not actually flies, but a type of beetle. The adults glow to find each other when they fly out at night, looking for a mate. Some can even flash on and off to send messages.

Many other sea creatures, including some sharks, squid, and jellyfish, also have glowing lights.

How it works

Bioluminescence happens when special types of chemicals combine inside an animal's body. They cause a chemical reaction that gives off light. Some creatures, like the Hawaiian squid, don't actually make their own light. Instead, they have glowing bacteria living inside their bodies. The bacteria make the light, acting like a lantern for the squid. In return, the squid feeds the bacteria and offers them a safe place to live.

Yikes!

In marshy, boggy places, you can sometimes see strange, flickering lights hovering around at night. People used to think they were ghosts or fairies, and called them "Will o' the wisps" or "spook lights." In fact, they come from gases bubbling up from the bog, mixing together, and catching fire.

Cats' eyes

At night, cats' eyes (above) seem to glow. However, they are not bioluminescent. They don't give out light, only reflect it. Cats, along with tigers, sharks, owls, and many other animals, have a silvery layer (like a mirror) at the back of each eye that reflects light. This makes the light hit the eye's light-detecting cells twice instead of once, helping cats to see well in the dark.

Deadly light

L ight gives us life, but too much of it in the wrong place or at the wrong time can be a serious problem. It can even be a killer—so beware!

Sizzling in the Sun

You probably know you should cover up your skin in the sunshine, or wear plenty of sunscreen. That's because the Sun's rays include ultraviolet light that can burn skin badly. Sunburn turns those with pale, sensitive skin bright red and makes it feel sore, blister, and peel off in flakes.

Not one of my better ideas...

Don't look!

You should never look directly at the Sun. Isaac Newton, not content with poking himself in the eye (see page 17), tried covering one eye and staring at the Sun for several minutes with the other. The vision in this eye began changing color, and was filled with spots and blobs. Newton had to rest in a dark room for several days before he could see properly again, and his eye was probably damaged for life.

Ouch!

Even worse than a sunburn, UV light can cause skin cancer, which is often deadly. Doctors treat it by chopping it out of the skin, but this doesn't always work and the cancer can spread.

Aaaarrrggh! My eyes!

Bright light can also cause headaches and temporary blindness, and has even been used as a method of torture. Polar and mountain explorers often wear snow goggles to cut out the glare of sunlight reflecting off the snow, as it can cause "snow blindness." Dazzling sunshine can also be hazardous for fighter pilots, so they wear helmets, like this one, with special eye shades.

Too bright for my brain

On TV, you sometimes hear a warning that flashing lights are about to appear. That's because they can be bad for people who have a brain disease called epilepsy. Photo flashes or flickering disco lights can trigger a dangerous epileptic fit, making the sufferer fall to the ground and tremble.

The future's bright

Scientists haven't finished experimenting with light. They're still working on new ways to use it, and exciting new light technologies.

Now you see me, now you don't!

At the moment, our attempts at becoming invisible are basic camouflage, such as these ones. Invisibility cloaks only exist in sci-fi stories and the pages of *Harry Potter*, but that is set to change. Scientists are working on ways to bend light around an object, so that it seems to disappear. One way of doing this uses optical fibers. Another idea is for a cloak or suit that videotapes what is going on behind it, then projects it towards the viewer.

A natural glow

Imagine a pet cat that glows in the dark! What about using glowing trees and plants instead of streetlights? Scientists have already found ways to copy genes (instructions found in cells) from glowing creatures, such as jellyfish, and add them to other living things like mice (left), to make them give off light. The reason? So they can see that the technique has actually worked! This **genetic engineering** could help people in the future with all sorts of diseases and illnesses.

Light power

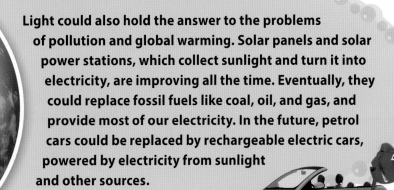

Light could also hold the answer to the problems of pollution and global warming. Solar panels and solar power stations, which collect sunlight and turn it into electricity, are improving all the time. Eventually, they could replace fossil fuels like coal, oil, and gas, and provide most of our electricity. In the future, petrol cars could be replaced by rechargeable electric cars, powered by electricity from sunlight and other sources.

 ## See for Yourself

Why are solar panels dark?

Take a sheet of black paper and a sheet of white paper, and tape them to a sunny window to soak up the sunlight. Leave them for five minutes, then test which is warmer. White surfaces reflect light and heat, while black surfaces are better at absorbing it. Solar panels are dark blue or black because it helps them to take in as much light as possible.

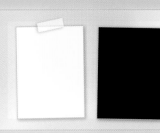

Laser weapons

In sci-fi films, bad guys have scary laser guns. Could they really exist? Some laser weapons have actually been made, but they use a lot of power and don't work very well. One type of non-deadly laser gun is being developed to control crowds. In the future, we could certainly see more of them.

Glossary

algae Simple plant-like things but without stems, roots, or leaves

bacteria Tiny single-celled living things

bioluminescence Light given off by living things

camera obscura Dark room where light enters through a tiny hole, making an upside-down image

camouflage Colors and patterns that allow something to blend into the background

electromagnetic spectrum (EMS) A range of different wavelengths of light energy

filament A thin thread or wire

gamma rays A dangerous type of light energy wave

genetic engineering Experimenting with genes

infrared light A form of light energy that we cannot see

laser A type of intense light in a narrow beam

lens A clear, curved object that bends light rays

light year The distance light travels in one year

optical fiber A flexible tube that light can travel along

microwave A type of light energy wave

nocturnal Active at night

Northern Lights Pattern of light in the sky, caused by particles from the Sun

photosynthesis The process plants use to build plant material using light energy

physics The science of forces, energy, and matter

prism A wedge-shaped, clear object that splits light into colors

pupil Hole in the eyeball that lets light in

reflection Light bouncing off a surface

refraction Light bending as it passes between different substances

retina Light-detecting area at the back of the eyeball

ultraviolet (UV) light A form of light energy that we cannot see

vitreous humor Clear jelly inside the eyeball

X-ray A type of light energy wave

Websites and Places to visit

Optics for Kids: Exploring the Science of Light
www.optics4kids.org/
Facts about light and light scientists, interesting activities and experiments, and amazing optical illusions to try.

Science Kids: Light
www.sciencekids.co.nz/light.html
Experiments, games, activities, and fun facts all to do with the science of light.

How the eye works
www.childrensuniversity.manchester.ac.uk/interactives/science/brainandsenses/eye/
Learn more about how we use our eyes to see.

HubbleSite
http://hubblesite.org/
Find out everything you could want to know about the Hubble Space Telescope, and view some of the amazing sights it has seen.

National Media Museum
Bradford,
West Yorkshire,
BD1 1NQ, UK
www.nationalmediamuseum.org.uk/

Canada Science and Technology Museum
1867 St. Laurent Blvd
Ottawa, Ontario K1G 5A3
Canada
www.sciencetech.technomuses.ca/

Exploratorium
3601 Lyon Street
San Francisco, CA 94123
U.S.A.
www.exploratorium.edu/

Museum of Science
1 Science Park
Boston, MA 02114
U.S.A.
www.mos.org/

Ontario Science Centre
770 Don Mills Road
Toronto, Ontario,
Canada
www.ontariosciencecentre.ca

Index

Ecosystems of North America

The Everglades and the Gulf Coast

Daniel Blaustein

BENCHMARK BOOKS

MARSHALL CAVENDISH
NEW YORK

Series Consultant: Stephen R. Kellert, Ph.D., School of Forestry and Environmental Studies, Yale University

Consultant: Richard Haley, Director, Goodwin Conservation Center

Benchmark Books
Marshall·Cavendish Corporation
99 White Plains Road
Tarrytown, New York 10591-9001

Library of Congress Cataloging-in-Publication Data
Blaustein, Daniel.
    The Everglades and the Gulf Coast / Daniel Blaustein.
       p.   cm.—(Ecosystems of North America)
    Includes bibliographical references and index.
    Summary: Presents an overview of wetland ecology as seen in Florida's Everglades, the largest
freshwater wetlands ecosystem in the continental United States.
    ISBN 0-7614-0896-7 (lib. bdg.)
    1. Wetland ecology—Florida—Everglades—Juvenile literature. 2. Wetland ecology—Gulf Coast
(U.S.)—Juvenile literature. [1. Everglades (Fla.) 2. Gulf Coast (U.S.) 3. Wetland ecology. 4. Ecology]
    I. Title II. Series.
QH104.5.G84B58   2000   97-38629
577.68'09759'39—dc21   CIP
                                                  AC

Photo Credits

The photographs in this book are used by permission and through the courtesy of:
Animals Animals/Earth Scenes: Patricia Caulfield 18; Stephen David Miller 20; Patti Murray 49;
R.F. Head 50. **_James Randklev:_** cover, back cover. **_Peter Arnold, Inc:_** Ed Reschke 4-5; Harvey Lloyd
8; Patricia Caulfield 16-17, 44-45; S.J. Kraseman 32; Clyde H. Smith 42; James A. Karales 46; John
Cancalosi 58. **_Slides Unlimited, Inc.:_** 52-53, 55. **_Tom Stack & Associates:_** Mark A. Stack 14; Brian
Parker 24-25, 40. **_Visuals Unlimited:_** Betty R. Strasser 10; Barbara Gerlach 12; William J. Weber 21, 36,
37, 48; Max and Bea Hunn 26; Joe McDonald 28; Charlie Heidecker 31; Marc Epstein 34-35; Kjell Sandved 38.
Cover design by Ann Antoshak for BBI.

Series Created and Produced by BOOK BUILDERS INCORPORATED

Printed in Hong Kong
6 5 4 3

Contents

Touring the Everglades and the Gulf Coast

Deep in the heart of Florida's Everglades, a wood stork stands motionless in the grassy water. Dense swarms of mosquitoes buzz all around. Dragonflies hover over the water's surface. Ducks dip into the water to nibble on water plants growing in the soft mud. It's midmorning, which means it is feeding time for many animals in the Everglades. With its eyes fixed on the dark water, the wood stork suddenly thrusts its long neck forward to catch a fish. Water splashes softly as an alligator lumbers out of the muck in search of a sunny place to rest. Startled, the stork spreads its great wings and lifts off the soggy marsh.

Welcome to the Everglades marsh, one of the wettest places on Earth! A marsh is a type of **wetland,** an area of land that is covered with water for all or part of the year. Marshes are fascinating places to learn about nature and how it works. In many ways, the Everglades is no different from other marshes within the Gulf Coast region of the United States. The states that lie along the Gulf of Mexico—Florida, Alabama,

The American alligator is one of the largest reptiles in the United States.

Mississippi, Louisiana, and Texas—are well known for their miles upon miles of wetlands and the impressive variety of living things found there. In fact, wetlands make up almost one-third of Florida and Louisiana. There are more wetlands in these two states than anywhere else in the continental United States.

Soggy, Wet, and Wonderful

Wetlands are just what the name says, "wet lands." Marshes and swamps are two types of wetlands. **Marshes** are wetlands characterized by the growth of nonwoody plants such as grasses. **Swamps** are forested wetlands filled with shrubs and hardwood trees, such as cypress. Wetlands can be found both inland and along the coast. Inland wetlands, such as the Everglades marsh and the cypress swamps, are freshwater wetlands. The water is supplied by rainfall and overflow from rivers and lakes. Wetlands found along the coast include the **mangrove swamps** and **salt marshes.** These are saltwater and brackish-water wetlands, which means they are covered by a mixture of freshwater and salt water. Trees grow in mangrove swamps on salty, muddy shores with their bases submerged in water. Thick grasses and grasslike plants cover the salt marshes.

In wetlands, water is the controlling factor in the environment. Here, the water level is constantly changing. Sometimes wetlands overflow. At other times, especially during the late summer, fall, and winter, wetlands can become completely dry. The wet season, a period of warm temperatures and high rainfall, begins in May and lasts through November. Although the dry season, from December through April, is still warm, there is much less rainfall.

Water is part of everyday life for the animals and plants that inhabit the marshes and swamps of the Everglades and the Gulf Coast. Water in the wetlands circulates endlessly, from the earth to the atmosphere and back again, in a process called the **water cycle.** Water evaporates from the surface of the earth, where it is held in oceans, lakes, swamps, marshes, rivers, soil, and living things.

Wetlands of the Everglades and the Gulf Coast

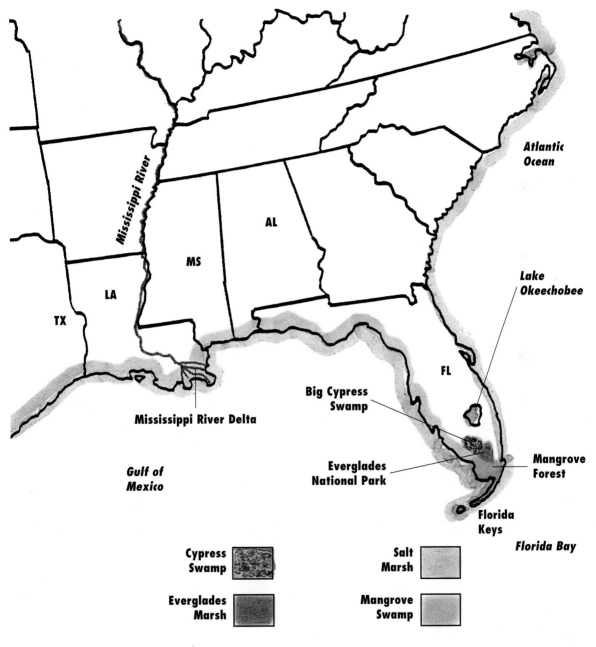

Atlantic Ocean

Mississippi River

AL

MS

LA

TX

Lake Okeechobee

FL

Big Cypress Swamp

Mississippi River Delta

Everglades National Park

Mangrove Forest

Gulf of Mexico

Florida Keys

Florida Bay

Cypress Swamp

Salt Marsh

Everglades Marsh

Mangrove Swamp

The wetlands of the Everglades and the Gulf Coast stretch from the southern tip of Florida westward to the southern tip of Texas.

After rising into the air as vapor, water eventually condenses into clouds and falls back to the earth as rain, snow, or other forms of **precipitation.** The great abundance of rainfall in the Everglades and the Gulf Coast community is the key to this area's incredible array of **species**, or kinds of plants and animals. Scientists refer to the variety of species within a region as its **biodiversity**.

Biodiversity in the Wetlands

Wetlands are full of life. Plants may be the most visible species, but wetlands also attract thousands of kinds of animals. Wetlands have a high biodiversity. In the United States alone, more than 5,000 species of plants, 270 kinds of birds, and nearly 200 different amphibians are found in wetlands.

All wetlands organisms are adapted to withstand very soggy conditions.

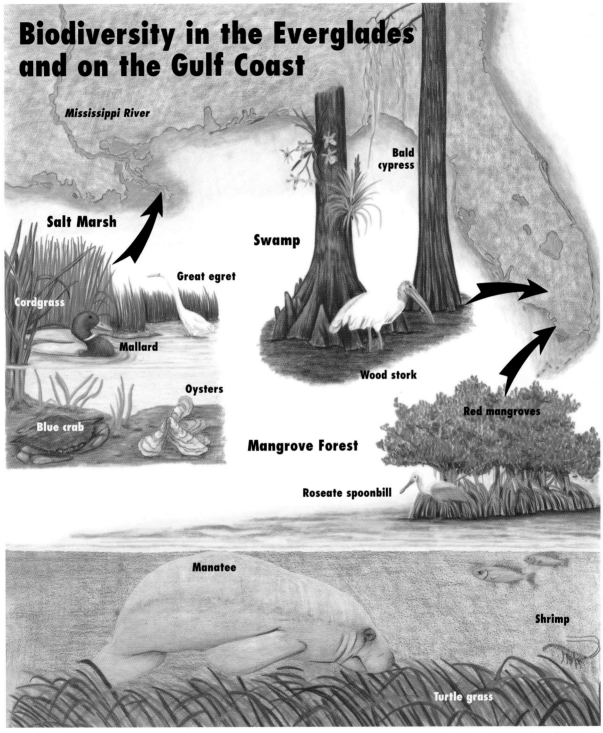

Biodiversity in the Everglades and on the Gulf Coast

Mississippi River

Bald cypress

Salt Marsh

Swamp

Great egret

Cordgrass

Mallard

Oysters

Wood stork

Blue crab

Red mangroves

Mangrove Forest

Roseate spoonbill

Manatee

Shrimp

Turtle grass

With so many different types of habitats, the diversity of organisms in the Everglades and on the Gulf Coast is very high.

Wetlands are favorite spots for ducks, geese, and long-legged cranes to stop on their long migration routes.

Why do wetlands have such great biodiversity? Wetlands support many different species because they provide a wealth of **habitats,** places that have all the living and nonliving things that an organism needs to live and grow. For instance, both terrestrial (land) and aquatic (water) animals can live in a marsh. The wet areas of the marsh support insects, fish, frogs, snails, and other creatures that need water to survive and reproduce. In turn, these creatures provide food for larger animals, such as birds, snakes, and raccoons, that live in the drier areas of the marsh. Geese, ducks, and other migratory birds stop here as well to feed on the tiny fish, shrimp, snails, and tender plants.

Wetlands are also found in other parts of North America, but the Everglades and the Gulf Coast have a greater variety of plants, insects, reptiles, birds, mammals, and other species than anywhere else in the continental United States. These particular wetlands are unique because they are the only wetlands on the continent with a nearly tropical climate. Temperatures remain warm and steady throughout the year, and rainfall is abundant. Because food, water, and shelter are plentiful, many species are able to thrive here.

The Web of Life

Organisms, or living things, inhabit many different **environments,** which include all the living and nonliving things that surround them and influence their lives. All the organisms that live together within a particular environment make up a **biological community.** Wetlands communities, such as the Everglades marsh, the cypress swamps, and the mangrove forests, are each filled with unique collections of plants and animals.

The organisms that make up each of these communities don't live in isolation. They're part of a much larger network called an **ecosystem,** which includes all living things in a biological community, as well as the nonliving elements with which organisms interact. Ecosystems can be as big as an ocean or as small as a drop of water.

How do ecosystems work? Like a computer, an ecosystem is made up of different parts that work together. A computer system will not function unless it has a keyboard, mouse, screen, and many other components. These different parts are interconnected. In a similar way, the living things in an ecosystem—the grasses, birds, and reptiles—interact with each other and with nonliving things, such as soil, sunlight, and water. Frogs eat insects, and fish eat tadpoles. Insects eat plants, as do some fish. To digest a meal, alligators and other cold-blooded creatures need to warm their bodies in sunlight. To catch a meal, crocodiles sometimes swallow stones in order to dive deeper.

Energy for Life

All organisms need energy in order to carry on all the basic life functions. Where does the energy come from? The sun is the original source of energy in ecosystems, but living things cannot use the sun's energy directly. Plants carry out **photosynthesis,** a process by which sunlight is used to make food. They are called **producers** because they produce energy, in the form of food, from sunlight. In this way, plants make energy available to other organisms.

For most living things, however, the immediate source of energy is the food they eat. Energy moves from one organism to another along a **food chain,** the feeding relationship in which one organism is eaten by another organism, which is, in turn, eaten by a larger one. Most ecosystems contain many different food chains.

The muskrat is one of the many links in the Everglades food chain. When animals eat plants or other animals, energy is passed on through the ecosystem.

Plants make up the first link on the food chain; the second link, **primary consumers**, are the animals that feed directly on plants. In the Everglades, muskrats, squirrels, birds, and a variety of insects all feed on plants. When larger animals feed on these smaller animals, energy is passed farther up the food chain. At the top of the food chain are the **predators.** These are animals such as snakes, alligators, and eagles that hunt and kill other animals for food.

A food chain traces the path of energy as it moves from one species to the next. But interactions among species are in reality more complex. Often food chains overlap, because most animals eat more than one type of food. When different species in a food chain interact with those of another chain, they become part of a **food web.** This web includes all of the interconnected food chains within an ecosystem.

Visitors to the Everglades and the Gulf Coast can see an amazing number of fascinating plants and animals. However, many people would consider a trek through a wetland to be an unpleasant experience. There is so much mud, and the air is filled with insects and an unmistakable odor, like rotten eggs. The strong, earthy odor is produced by millions of microscopic creatures that are busy carrying out important jobs. These unseen workers—mainly bacteria and fungi—are known as **decomposers.** Decomposers get their energy by breaking down dead organisms into smaller particles and feeding on them. By doing this, decomposers clean up waste in the ecosystem. They recycle essential nutrients, such as water, carbon, oxygen, nitrogen, and phosphorus, back into the environment in a form that can be used again by growing plants.

Lasting Value

Sometimes we forget that like animals and plants, people interact in some way with almost everything in the environment. From our surroundings, we obtain food, water, minerals, lumber, oil, and other resources.

Wetlands are extremely valuable to human life. Long before there were grocery stores, wetlands were places where people could

A weekend fishing trip to the Everglades and the Gulf Coast poses little threat to the habitat. Commercial fishing, on the other hand, may lead to overharvesting of the rich waters.

gather food. Rice, cranberries, water chestnuts, and mint come from wetlands plants. Wetlands yield fish for the nation. In fact, many of the fish, crabs, clams, oysters, and shrimp that we eat are harvested from the Everglades and the Gulf Coast.

Wetlands also help to improve the quality of the environment we live in. For example, as water passes through a wetland, the plants filter it. Microorganisms such as bacteria break down the contaminants. The water emerges cleaner and eventually runs into lakes, rivers, and oceans. In addition, wetlands help control flooding. Acting like natural tubs or sponges, wetlands store water and slowly release it back into the environment.

Trees and other vegetation in wetlands also work to slow floodwaters. For example, coastal wetlands, such as Florida's mangrove forests, prevent flooding by blocking high waves that batter the state's coastline. Mangrove forests can even help stabilize soils and create new land. Today, mangrove trees are being planted in many parts of Florida to help prevent shoreline **erosion,** the wearing away of land by natural forces such as wind and water.

Wetlands are also used for recreation—for nature photography, waterfowl hunting, fishing, and boating. However, the great appeal of these areas has also put them at risk. Resources are depleted through overhunting and overfishing. And many mangrove forests, which grow along coveted ocean shores, are being destroyed to make room for hotels and other buildings.

As people begin to realize the importance of maintaining wetlands for our continued use and enjoyment, more efforts are directed at preserving them. Learning about the wetlands—how they affect us and how we, in turn, affect them—is a first step in appreciating their value. We will begin by exploring the Everglades marsh, a very delicate wetlands ecosystem. We will then turn to the forested, freshwater cypress swamps and the oceanside mangrove forests, followed by a look at the soggy world of the salt marshes.

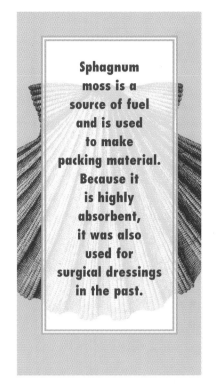

Sphagnum moss is a source of fuel and is used to make packing material. Because it is highly absorbent, it was also used for surgical dressings in the past.

River of Grass

The Everglades marsh, located in south Florida, is a vast wetlands ecosystem made up of marshes and swamps. It is sometimes called a river of grass. It's easy to see why. Viewed from the air, the Everglades appears to be miles and miles of shallow water flowing through thick mats of grass. Nearly 50 miles (81 km) across and 110 miles (177 km) long, the Everglades does flow like a river. But unlike a river, it flows so incredibly slowly that from a distance it wouldn't seem to move at all.

The Everglades begins at Lake Okeechobee, a large lake in the center of Florida, and ends in the Gulf of Mexico and Florida Bay. Almost 70 percent of the plant life in this ecosystem is made up of the sawgrass plant. Because of its rows of tiny, sharp teeth, which grow along the edges of its leaves, sawgrass can cut right through a person's clothing and skin! Just as people need proper protection when walking through sawgrass, these plants need their tiny teeth to protect them from being eaten.

Razor sharp sawgrass is the most common plant in the Everglades' river of grass.

Water Matters

All of the wildlife in the Everglades is totally dependent on the cycling of water. Look, for example, at the interesting feeding relationship between the snail kite, an endangered bird species, and the apple snail. The rainy season is a time of reproduction for the apple snail, a freshwater mollusk the size of a golf ball. When water levels are at their highest, apple snails lay thousands of tiny pink eggs on the stalks of marsh grasses.

During the wet season, snail kites fly all over the Everglades looking for the abundant apple snails. These birds were named snail kites because they will swoop down from the air when they spot a cluster of mature apple snails. They have specialized beaks, perfectly designed for plucking the tender snails from their shells.

The fragile apple snail is the main food of the endangered snail kite.

The water cycle, a process basic to every ecosystem, and the lives of apple snails and snail kites are intertwined. Snail kites depend on the successful reproduction of apple snails, which is, in turn, affected by the amount of rainfall. Only recently have scientists been able to observe how close this relationship is. When humans drained large areas of the Everglades and converted them to agricultural lands, the population of apple snails decreased sharply. This had a dramatic effect on the snail kite population. Fewer than nine hundred snail kites remain in Florida, the bird's only U.S. habitat. The relationship among humans, snail kites, and apple snails illustrates the delicate balance of nature in an ecosystem. As we'll see again later, when humans alter the water cycle, they directly affect the food chain.

One of the most important books ever written about the Everglades was *Everglades, River of Grass* by Marjory Stoneman Douglas. Published in 1947, the book focused public attention on the environmental problems of the Everglades and explained why the Everglades were worth saving.

Life in a Gator Hole

Alligators are animals that often come to mind when people think of the Everglades. The American alligator, once a highly endangered reptile, plays a critical role in the Everglades ecosystem, especially during the dry season. As winter approaches, water levels begin to drop. Alligators, which need an ample supply of water to survive, sense the changing of the season and begin to prepare for the dry months ahead. Using their powerful snouts, tails, and legs, alligators make comfortable dens for themselves by slashing sawgrass, small plants, and muck out of the marsh. As the alligator thrashes its body from side to side, it creates a small hole filled with water. Plant matter and mud piled up around the edges of the hole create dry ground on which other plants eventually grow. After many years, grass, trees, and other plants surround these "gator holes" like fences.

Gator holes are important to other species as well. As the marsh water becomes scarce during the dry season, many animals search for food and remaining pockets of water. The gator holes attract crayfish, frogs, turtles, fish, and other aquatic species, all

The alligator is considered a keystone species in the Everglades because so many other animals depend upon it for their survival.

seeking refuge in the deeper waters of the gator holes. Muskrats, otters, deer, and raccoons, as well as a wide variety of beautiful birds, including ibises, egrets, and herons, visit these sanctuaries to feed on the small animals that can be found there.

The busy alligators have earned the nickname "keepers of the glades." Because alligators and the watery hollows they make play such an important role in the Everglades ecosystem, they are considered to be a **keystone species**: many other species depend upon them for their survival.

Keeping a Delicate Balance

Due to constantly changing water levels, wetlands ecosystems like the Everglades can be *very* unpredictable places. Since the 1800s, people have tried to control the Everglades to prevent flooding. To drain away the water, large canals were built to send the water into the ocean and away from the Everglades. The land along the canals dried and became more useful to people. Today, about half of the original Everglades has been drained to create dry land for towns and farms. However, this development has had a disastrous effect on many species, as in the case of the shrinking population of snail kites.

Before so much of the Everglades was drained, most of its water came from Lake Okeechobee, which sometimes overflowed along its southern edge. With an annual rainfall of nearly 60 inches (152 cm) and the overflow from the lake, a large area of the Everglades used to be wet for most of the year. But the lake was also a source of major flooding to towns, especially during the rainy season.

In the 1920s, other flood control projects were started, including the construction of a dike along Lake Okeechobee's southern rim. Because water no longer overflowed from the lake, farmers, ranchers, and city dwellers now had more dry land on which to live and work. More projects followed in the 1940s and 1950s. Much of the region is now crisscrossed by an elaborate system of canals, dikes, and levees.

A network of large canals in south Florida helps control flooding by channeling large amounts of water from the Everglades to the ocean.

Water control efforts have benefited people in south Florida. But now nature no longer controls the flow of water into the Everglades; people do. As a result, the natural balance of the ecosystem has been damaged. Many animals that depend on water for reproduction, such as snails, fish, and frogs, have been harmed by the draining of the Everglades. And because these creatures lie at the base of many Everglades food chains, their diminishing numbers have had a rippling effect throughout the entire community. Like the snail kite, other bird species, such as the ibis, heron, and the endangered wood stork, have suffered as well. In fact, scientists have estimated that some bird populations have dropped about 90 percent over the past fifty years because of the low water levels. Now scientists are encouraging us to realize that a great number of plants and animals must survive to help maintain this delicate environment.

From Marshland to Farmland

Because the canals and dikes have helped to dry up the land, part of the original Everglades has become a rich agricultural area. Yet, productivity within this marsh has had a negative effect on its wildlife. In the 1950s and 1960s, bald eagles and pelicans in the Everglades were among the many birds threatened with **extinction,** or complete disappearance from the earth, by the chemical DDT. Farmers sprayed DDT on their crops to control insects. They didn't realize that **runoff** —overflow of water—from heavy rains was washing the poisonous chemical into the Everglades. Scientists discovered that DDT caused the shells of birds' eggs to thin, resulting in the death of many young birds before hatching. The U.S. government finally banned the use of DDT in 1972.

Agricultural runoff disrupts the Everglades ecosystem in other ways too. Fertilizers, which contain plant nutrients, are washed from

At the turn of the century, people imported a plant called melaleuca from Australia to help control flooding in the Everglades. Like many wetlands plants, melaleuca absorbs large amounts of water. Unfortunately, it grows quickly and crowds out native plants. After scientists discovered that melaleuca was destroying important plants in the Everglades, they gave it the nickname Everglades Terminator.

the sugarcane plantations north of the river of grass. In the Everglades, fertilizers cause an excessive growth of tiny microscopic plants called algae. The algae can form large mats called **algal blooms,** which float on the surface of the water. This results in **eutrophication,** a process by which bodies of water become thick with vegetation. The effects of eutrophication can be seen as far south as Florida Bay, on the southernmost edge of the Everglades. As the algae die and decompose, they use up large amounts of oxygen in the water. As a result, fish, crabs, shrimp, insects, and other aquatic species suffocate in the oxygen-depleted water.

With the drier conditions created in the Everglades, brush fires began to sweep through the Everglades in the 1930s and 1940s. These devastating blazes led environmentalists to pressure the government to establish the Everglades National Park. Today, visitors can experience Florida's diverse, rare, and beautiful wild-life in the Everglades National Park. Located in the southwestern portion of the marsh, this is one of the largest national parks in the United States. Each year, millions of tourists come to see the vast array of tropical wildlife, which includes nearly six hundred different types of animals, such as alligators, crocodiles, pelicans, snakes, and a multitude of insect species.

Land Underwater

If you travel west from the grassy part of the Everglades, you'll encounter Big Cypress Swamp, another active community within the larger Everglades ecosystem. A cypress swamp is a type of forested, freshwater wetland.

After sawgrass, the most dominant plants in the Everglades are trees. More than 120 different kinds, with such unusual names as pond apple, swamp bay, and wax myrtle, can be found here. Some of them grow on small elevated patches of land that rise 1 to 2 feet (31–61 cm) above the surface of the grassy waterways. Hundreds of these teardrop-shaped islands, or hammocks, are scattered throughout the Everglades.

In cypress swamps, cypress trees, draped with moss, ferns, and other plants, dominate the landscape, standing firmly in the dark and shallow swamp water. The spreading branches of these giant trees form a canopy that blocks out most sunlight. The few patches of solid earth are packed with dense tangles of vegetation. How can plants and animals live in such a crowded, dimly lit, and thoroughly soggy place?

The bald cypress is related to the sequoia tree, and cypress swamps are wetlands forests that are found in Florida and other Gulf Coast states.

Cypress swamps are not only found in the Everglades but also along the Gulf Coast in Florida, Alabama, Mississippi, Louisiana, and Texas. With their dazzling displays of unique plants and animals, these swamps are excellent places to study the **adaptations**, or special features, of species to wetlands. Adaptation is the key to survival in these crowded and waterlogged lands.

Cypress trees are often called "trees with knees" because of the knobby growths that emerge from the roots of the trees.

Trees with Knees

The most obvious species that is well adapted to the cypress swamps is the giant cypress tree, particularly the bald cypress. Cypress trees are closely related to pine trees. However, they are not evergreen like pines. Rather, the bald cypress is deciduous, which means it loses its needles in the fall. It is primarily a southern tree that thrives in warm, humid climates. The cypress is among the world's longest living trees. Some trees in Big Cypress Swamp are more than 600 years old. In some places, they have lived to be 2,000!

If you look at the base of a bald cypress, you will notice that it appears swollen. This adaptation is common in wetlands trees because these bulging bases help trees stand in the soft, wet soil. Cypress trees have another unique feature that has earned them the nickname "trees with knees." This refers to their unusual root system, which is always submerged in water. The "knees" are knobby and twisted outgrowths that protrude from the roots and stick up out of the shallow water. Although the exact purpose of the knees isn't fully understood, some scientists believe they may actually help the tree breathe and cope with the low oxygen levels in the root zone.

Air It Out

Have you ever seen a plant growing in the air? If you visit Big Cypress Swamp, you'll likely see many varieties of these air plants, or epiphytes. Epiphytes don't really grow in air, but they can be found growing hundreds of feet up on the immense branches of the cypress tree. In cypress swamps, growing space on the ground is limited. Dry land is scarce, and sunlight filters to the swamp floor in scattered patches. Epiphytes have literally taken to the trees to escape the dark and soggy swamp floor.

Spanish moss, which hangs from tree branches in thick mats, is a common epiphyte in the cypress swamp, as are the colorful and fragrant orchids that grow on the trees. Epiphytes have no need for roots and soil but get their moisture and nutrients from the air. Many people mistakenly think that epiphytes are parasites and harm the trees on which they grow. Actually, epiphytes are just "renting" space so that they can have a place in the sun. The

Epiphytes, such as this bromeliad, don't harm the plants they grow on. They simply borrow space to grow.

relationship between epiphytes and cypress trees is called **commensalism.** In this type of interaction, one species benefits without harming the other.

Bromeliads, another common epiphyte, play an important role in the cypress swamps. Members of the pineapple family, some bromeliads have long, overlapping leaves that form cups for holding water during the dry season. The cups provide habitats for many living things. When the cups are filled with water, they offer safe havens where mosquitoes and other insects can lay their eggs. Frogs, salamanders, snakes, and other small animals that make their homes in the tall cypress trees also use the bromeliads as temporary watering holes. Even birds and raccoons look to bromeliads for a drink during the dry winter months.

How Much Water Can Moss Hold?

Many wetlands plants have amazing water-holding properties, which help control flooding. People claim that sphagnum moss, a common freshwater wetlands plant, can hold 10 times its weight in water. Try the following activity to find out how much water sphagnum moss can actually hold.

1. Obtain three small samples of living sphagnum moss from a local nursery. Pieces of moss about 2 inches (5 cm) in length should be fine.

2. Shake off excess dirt and water from the moss samples then weigh on a scale. Record the weights.

3. Squeeze the pieces of moss together in your hand to force out the air. Next, submerge the moss samples in a large container of water and let them expand. Leave the moss underwater for about five minutes.

4. Weigh the moss samples again. Record the new weights.

5. Use the following formula to determine how much water the moss held:

   Weight of wet moss – Weight of dry moss = Weight of water held by moss

6. Use the following formula to find out how times its weight in water the moss holds:

   Weight of water in moss ÷ Weight of dry moss = X

For the Birds

Whereas cypress swamps are home to an impressive variety of animals, including bears, panthers, lizards, fish, and countless species of insects, they are a virtual paradise for birds. Tropical wading birds— egrets, herons, and ibises—thrive here. Wading birds are species that slowly wade into shallow water to catch fish, tadpoles, insects, and other small aquatic animals. All wading birds have long, spindly legs, an adaptation that helps them prop their bodies above the water. They also have long, pointed or curved beaks for catching their prey.

Bird lovers are drawn to Big Cypress Swamp, the site of the largest breeding ground in the Everglades for the wood stork, a wading bird with a five-foot (2-m) wingspan. Locally known as flintheads because of their gray heads, wood storks nest in enormous numbers in cypress trees.

Like other wading birds, wood storks are well adapted to the constantly changing water levels in the cypress swamps. They are also highly dependent on them. In fact, experts at the Everglades National Park consider the wood stork to be a good indicator of the health of the entire Everglades system. When the wood stork population drops, scientists know there is an imbalance within the ecosystem. Wood storks nest at the same time every year, when water levels begin to drop in the winter. As the swamps dry up, water collects in tiny pools. Wood storks depend on these little water holes because they supply the fish needed to feed their young. Wood storks will often fly 30 to 40 miles (48–64 km) in search of a pool brimming with fish.

Wood storks are the most endangered wading bird in the ecosystem. In the 1930s, some four thousand breeding pairs of wood storks nested in the Everglades. Today, fewer than one hundred breeding pairs remain. Most agree that the number of birds began to decline when people started altering water levels in the Everglades. Managed water levels delay the natural drying up of the swamps.

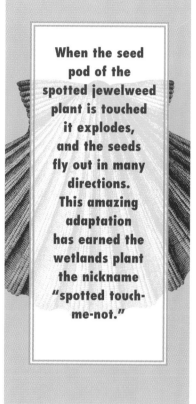

When the seed pod of the spotted jewelweed plant is touched it explodes, and the seeds fly out in many directions. This amazing adaptation has earned the wetlands plant the nickname "spotted touch-me-not."

Wood storks, once very common in the Everglades ecosystem, have been seriously threatened by flood control.

This causes the wood storks to begin nesting much too late in the winter. When the spring rains come, the water holes fill up and disappear, scattering the wood storks' ample food supply. Many scientists fear that if this pattern continues, it may cause the extinction of wood storks. The decline of wood storks and other wading birds is one of the great problems facing modern **ecologists**, scientists who study the relationships among species and their environment.

Then and Now

Because cypress swamps are not only a valuable resource but also home to a vast number of endangered animal and plant species, ecologists worry about the threat our actions pose for the future of swamps. People have been worried about the plight of the Everglades and its wading birds ever since the turn of the century. In the early 1900s, egrets and spoonbills, which remain highly endangered birds today, were the focus of concern. In the 1880s and 1890s, the white and pink feathers of egrets and spoonbills were

Most egrets live near water, feeding on the fish, frogs, and other animals found there.

highly prized decorations for women's hats. To cash in on the new fashion craze, hunters ventured into the cypress swamps to shoot "long whites" and "short whites," as egrets were known in the trade. Suddenly, a new industry had blossomed in southern Florida. By 1900, the populations of egrets and spoonbills had been nearly wiped out.

Fortunately, the Florida Audubon Society began focusing public attention on the slaughter of wading birds. As a result, the drastic decline of egrets and spoonbills in the Everglades began to level off. Organized in 1900, the Florida Audubon Society works to protect Florida's wildlife and habitats through education, research, and political action. It has been successful in preserving many rare species. In fact, by the 1930s, pressure from the Florida Audubon Society and other environmental groups helped return entire populations of birds in the cypress swamps to pre-hunting levels. During the 1940s, however, the cypress swamps in Florida and those along the Gulf Coast faced a new threat—logging.

Bald cypress trees, which make excellent building materials, have long been in great demand. The tree is known as "wood everlasting" because of its ability to resist decay. During World War II, thousands of trainloads of cypress trees were cut from the cypress swamps and shipped north to be used as lumber for shipbuilding. Logging can cause habitat loss, the destruction or removal of a place where an organism lives. It is regarded as the single greatest threat to wildlife, particularly to endangered species. When trees are cut down and removed, the number of habitats available to species is reduced.

Because ecologists today recognize the significant threat of logging to wildlife, thousands of acres of cypress swamp in Florida, Mississippi, and Louisiana are now off limits to loggers. In areas that are not protected from logging, young cypress trees are immediately replanted to replace the ones that are removed. An old concern is growing into a modern effort to maintain this valuable landscape.

Thirty different varieties of snakes may be found in cypress swamps. Two of the largest are the cottonmouth (or water moccasin) and the eastern diamondback rattlesnake. Both are venomous snakes in the viper family.

Forests by the Sea

*P*icture a place that is neither land nor sea, where dolphins and manatees swim in crystal-clear waters, while raccoons and muskrats catch fiddler crabs within a thick tangle of tree roots. This wetlands community is unlike anything else found in North America. It is the mangrove swamp, a unique forest nurtured not by the land, but by the sea.

Mangrove swamps dominate the coast of southern Florida. They extend from Florida Bay at the southern tip of Florida and along its western coast on the Gulf of Mexico. These mangrove swamps are wetlands that lie in **estuaries,** places where the freshwater of rivers and streams meets and mixes with the salt water of the ocean. In Florida's mangrove swamps, the water is a mixture of freshwater from the Everglades and ocean water from the Atlantic and the Gulf. Estuaries serve as breeding grounds for the many kinds of plants and animals that require just the right balance of freshwater and salt water.

Mangrove swamps, where freshwater and salt water meet, are important nurseries for fish, insects, crabs, shrimp, and other crustaceans.

March of the Mangroves

Mangrove trees are salt-tolerant plants that grow along the coast-lines of many tropical and subtropical areas of the world. Because they can grow in both freshwater and salt water, they dominate tropical coastlines. Here, they have little competition, because few other plant species can stand the constant spray of salt from the wind and waves.

There are three different types of mangrove trees in the Everglades and the Gulf Coast—red, black, and white. Whereas salt can be deadly to many types of plants, it doesn't hurt the unusual mangrove tree. White mangroves grow the farthest inland, where the water is still mostly fresh. A little closer to the shore are the black mangroves. Black mangroves are more tolerant of salt than white mangroves. During high tide, the thick, woody roots of black

The seeds of the red mangrove develop and mature before they fall off the tree. This gives the young mangrove a better chance at surviving the salty conditions of life in the swamp.

mangroves are engulfed by the salty ocean water. To help its roots breathe better in the salty water, a black mangrove tree sends up little strawlike roots called pneumatophores, which suck oxygen from the air.

The most unusual type of mangrove tree is the red mangrove, which grows directly on the shoreline and often in the ocean itself. To survive, red mangroves have long, spindly, stilt-roots that anchor them firmly in the mud and prop them up out of the water. These long, twisted roots also help the trees draw oxygen from the air. Looking like long-legged spiders standing on tiptoe, red mangroves are perfectly suited to life near the ocean.

Red mangroves have adapted to life in and around salt water in other ways too. The flowers of red mangrove trees produce large, cigar-shaped seeds about 6 to 12 inches (15–31 cm) long. Instead of falling off the tree when they become mature, these fleshy seeds begin to grow into seedlings while still attached to the tree. When they fall, they poke into the soft mud and sprout roots within a day or two. Seeds that don't land directly in the mud may be carried away by the tides, sometimes to very distant shores. Mangrove seeds are hardy travelers. With a thick, waxy coating and an ample supply of stored food, a red mangrove seedling may travel for thousands of miles before landing in another area suitable for growth.

A Living Umbrella

Mangrove trees are the most visible species in this swamp ecosystem. The trees crowd the shoreline, and their roots intertwine to form a dense tangled mass. Except for the trees and some birds, mangrove forests appear lifeless. But these swamps are actually teeming with life. Hidden from the naked eye, within the tangle of mangrove roots, is a lively community that forms the base of a very complex food chain. In some ways, mangrove roots are a miniature ecosystem all their own. They form a kind of living umbrella that provides a habitat for a multitude of species.

Trees that grow in cooler climates, like maple and oak trees, bloom in the spring and lose all their leaves in the fall. Mangrove

37

Disruptions in the habitats of even the smallest organisms impact the entire food chain.

leaves, however, sprout and die a few at a time. When the leaves splash into the water, tides carry them back to the shoreline, where they collect and gather inside the tangled tree roots. Almost immediately, microscopic creatures like bacteria, protozoans, and fungi attack the leaves, breaking them down into a foul-smelling slime. Over time, layers of slime build up, forming a new land surface where mangrove trees sprout and grow.

Unappealing as it may sound, the slime attracts hungry hordes of worms and tiny crustaceans that feed on the rotting bits of leaves, decomposing them even further. These in turn become food for other creatures, such as snails, oysters, fiddler crabs, and shrimp. When tides are low, animals such as raccoons, muskrats, and birds raid the mangrove forests and gorge themselves on the ample food.

The Breeding Ground for Many

The crystal-clear waters of the mangrove swamp are calm and shallow. This is because mangrove trees are wave breakers; they reduce the force of the large ocean waves that crash against the coastline.

By breaking the waves, mangrove swamps protect the coast from the damaging effects of erosion. Scientists have found that mangrove trees actually help build up the coastline. In the calm waters of the mangrove swamp, sediments such as fine mud and sand accumulate. These growing layers of soft sediment create the perfect environment for the growth of new mangrove plants.

The rotting leaves of the mangrove turn into slime—a feeding ground for worms and tiny crustaceans.

As this process continues, several hundred feet of new mangrove forest are added to the coastline every year.

The calm waters of the mangrove swamp provide the perfect breeding ground for a great many species. Marine animals, such as shrimp, fish, crabs, clams, and oysters, lay hundreds of thousands of eggs in Florida's mangrove swamps. The warm waters of the estuary form a protective nursery that offers new hatchlings their best chance of survival. Insects also take advantage of the mangrove swamp's still waters. If you visit the Everglades at dusk, you will get a good idea about how diverse the insect life is here. Mosquitoes and gnats often gather in dense swarms at dusk, searching for unsuspecting animals to feed on. These familiar pests will travel for miles in search of a blood meal. Insects are abundant in all wetlands ecosystems because so many insect species need water to reproduce. An impressive variety of insects, including dragonflies, mosquitoes, gnats, horse flies, deer flies, and water beetles, lay their eggs in mangrove swamps.

Submerged plants also serve a purpose in the Everglades estuaries. Numerous grasses and seaweeds grow on the sandy bottom just offshore. Here, the dense beds of bright green turtle grass attract one of the world's most endangered mammals—the manatee, or sea cow. This large, plant-eating mammal is a popular attraction in Florida, where it spends the winter months. Manatees can be easily spotted gliding slowly up and down the south Florida shoreline. They feed only on sea plants and have a voracious appetite for turtle grass. In Florida, manatees help keep vital waterways clear of choking vegetation.

Mosquitoes breed in tremendous numbers in wetlands. About 43 different species have been identified in Everglades National Park alone. Mosquitoes thrive here because there is plenty of water for larvae to develop. Mosquitoes may be pests, but they are also an important link in the food chain, providing nutrition for fish, birds, bats, and dragonflies.

Upsetting the Balance

For much of this century, Florida has experienced tremendous population growth. Millions of tourists and thousands of new

The manatee, or sea cow, is a large, slow-moving animal found in the Gulf Coast, as well as in South America.

residents each year flock to its warm climate, tropical gardens, white sand beaches, and theme parks. Along the coastline, where mangroves grow, people are attracted by the clear waters, tropical vegetation, and rare animals. Waterfront property is in great demand. People benefit too from the foods mangrove swamps provide. Snapper, redfish, and snook are only a few of the fish that use these estuaries as breeding grounds and help fuel Florida's enormous seafood industry.

Despite the great beauty and important ecological roles of the mangrove swamps, these wetlands have long been thought of as wasted space. Over the years, as Florida's population has increased, thousands of acres of mangrove trees have been removed to make room for roads, office buildings, condominiums, and hotels.

With the removal of mangrove plants along the coast, the beaches and coastal resorts are clean and almost bug-free. However, the destruction of the mangrove forest ecosystem has had a disastrous effect on the huge number of animals and plants that live here. Many animals, particularly birds, have been forced out of their normal feeding spots and breeding grounds. And the increase in motor boats and recreational vehicles has also placed many sea animals in danger. For example, the slow-moving sea manatees live at great risk. Many are injured and killed each year by careless boaters.

As in all ecosystems, disruption of one part of an ecosystem can upset the balance of the whole. Fewer mangrove plants means less food and habitat for small mangrove animals. In turn, there is less food available for the larger birds, fish, muskrats, and raccoons, which feed on these smaller animals. And so it goes up the food chain. Florida's mangrove swamps have been damaged further by changes in the Everglades' river of grass. Disruptions in the natural flow of freshwater through the Everglades have upset the stable mixture of salt and freshwater on which mangroves and other plants depend. As a result, the mangroves have begun to die off, reducing the habitat and food supply for many species.

Scientists have started a number of projects in hopes of preserving the delicate mangrove swamps for years to come. The Marine Resources Council of South Florida is one of several groups

On August 24, 1992, Hurricane Andrew ripped through the Everglades and devastated a large portion of south Florida. Houses, buildings, and at least 70,000 acres (28,329 ha) of mangrove forest were devastated by Andrew's powerful winds. Today, the mangrove forests, which were uprooted by the fierce winds reaching up to 200 miles (320 km) per hour, have almost returned to their original condition.

addressing the problem. With the help of the U.S. National Marine Fisheries Service, the Council has mounted a concentrated effort to replant native mangroves along the coast and reestablish the functioning mangrove communities so essential to us all.

Many mangrove forests that once flourished along much of the coastline have been removed to make room for Florida's booming tourist industry.

Soggy Shorelines

*I*f you travel the roads along America's Gulf Coast, you are likely to see plenty of salt marsh. Salt marshes are coastal wetlands that form most often in places where freshwater rivers and streams meet up with the sea. Along the Gulf Coast, where rivers such as the Mississippi empty into the Gulf of Mexico, there are miles of salt marsh. But salt marshes are delicate ecosystems that cannot exist just anywhere along a shoreline. Salt marshes are found only in bays, lagoons, and other protected coastlines where waves are small. It is impossible for salt marshes to develop along exposed seashores. Even medium-sized waves would destroy their fragile structure.

Salt marshes form as a product of moving water. For example, rivers, streams, and ocean tides carry sediments—tiny particles of mud and clay—as they flow. Where the rivers and streams reach the sea, the sediments are deposited, and vast **mud flats** form. As the mud flats grow in size, they slowly become inhabited by plants and animals. Among the first species to inhabit new mud flats are algae. Algae grow to form a living carpet on the mud flats and set the stage for other creatures to move in.

Birds, such as the heron, feast on the abundance of life drawn to the salt marshes.

Pretty soon snails, crabs, shrimp, and birds are attracted to the flats and begin to feast on the algae. Over time other plants such as cord grass take hold in the thickening mud. Salt marsh cord grass, sometimes called *Spartina*, attracts still more animals, and eventually a salt marsh develops.

Salt marshes are places of extreme conditions. At high tide, the salt marsh is submerged in salty ocean water. At low tide, parts of the salt marsh are baked dry in the sun. Plants and animals must survive in an environment that changes twice daily with the rise and fall of the tides.

To cope with the salt and the fluctuating water levels, animals like snails and crabs adapt by burrowing in the mud or crawling on plant stems during high tide. Others, especially plants, have adaptations that help them tolerate the very salty conditions of the marsh.

Cord grass is a salt-loving plant, also known as a halophyte.

Hidden Worlds

When you first set foot on a salt marsh, you will not see much wildlife, except for a few snails, fiddler crabs, and the hordes of mosquitoes and flies that buzz around you. But more plants live and die in a salt marsh than in almost any other kind of environment. Gulf Coast salt marshes are especially productive.

You will see, for example, marsh grasses, glasswort, sea lavender, and bayberry, whose berries perfume soaps and candles. While these plants are different, they all have one thing in common—an ability to tolerate salt.

Salt-tolerant plants are called halophytes. The most common halophyte found in salt marshes is salt marsh cord grass, a type of marsh grass with very stiff, pointed leaves. Cord grasses live close to the shore and can withstand high levels of salt in the environment. Cord grasses are very tall, reaching up to 7 feet (2 m), yet during high tides they are often completely submerged in water. Special glands in the stems and leaves help the grass get rid of excess salt absorbed by the roots. At low tide it is often possible to see tiny salt crystals on the outside of the leaves.

The plants in a Gulf Coast salt marsh grow very fast and decay soon after they die. You might think that with the abundant plant life, the cord grass would be the main food for salt marsh animals. But cord grass is very difficult to digest, and only a few species, such as fiddler crabs, muskrats, and grass shrimp, can eat it directly. Instead, the cord grass is mostly consumed by bacteria and other decomposers. The natural process of decay, or decomposition, is at work in all wetlands ecosystems, helping to feed its population.

Muskrats, fiddler crabs, and grass shrimp help out bacteria by chewing the cord grass into small bits. When dead plants and animals decompose, nutrients are recycled back into the soil and water and help new plants grow. The process of decomposition occurs more rapidly in salt marshes than in other wetlands. The salt water helps to soften the tough cord grass, and constant tidal movement helps break down the plants even further. As a result, the entire marsh is constantly bathed in a type of fertilizing "soup" as the nutrients are recirculated by tides.

Animals such as the fiddler crab help the decomposition process in the salt marsh by tearing marsh plants into smaller bits.

Food for All?

The relationship between wetlands and human civilization dates back thousands of years. Some of the earliest-known human settlements, including those of prehistoric cultures in Europe and North America, were built around wetlands. Most were established along the coasts near estuaries and salt marshes because food and water were plentiful. People began to depend on the wetlands' many resources, such as food, water, and a variety of plant materials that could be used to make clothes, baskets, and other products. It shouldn't be surprising to find that throughout history many salt marshes and estuaries have been overfished, dumped on, drained, and filled to make room for new homes and buildings.

These days, the draining and filling of salt marshes and estuaries for urban structures is a major cause of the disappearance of wetlands. Those that aren't filled or drained are often harmed by pollution from nearby development. Rainwater washes pesticides, fertilizer, oil, and other pollutants from lawns and parking lots into marshes and estuaries on the coast. As a result, many animals and plants have lost their homes or have been poisoned. For example, migratory birds, such as the common tern, have been especially affected by the destruction of the Gulf Coast salt marshes. These birds now have a limited number of places to breed and feed their young during the cold winter months.

With the disappearance of the wetlands, the tern has difficulty finding places to feed its young, especially in colder weather.

People often forget how many wetlands resources they actually consume. Probably the most important resource from the Gulf Coast estuaries and salt marshes is seafood. The constant movement of the tides delivers rich nutrients into the ecosystem and helps provide nourishment for shrimp, crabs, lobsters, clams, oysters, and fish. In the United States alone, over $10 billion worth of fish and shellfish, much of it from the salt marshes and estuaries of the Gulf Coast region, are harvested every year.

Increased demand for fish and shellfish has placed a strain on the Gulf Coast salt marshes. Seafood is being harvested faster than it can be replaced. People fishing in the Gulf Coast region

Salt marshes along the Gulf Coast provide much of the fish and shellfish sold throughout the country.

have observed a drastic decline in the populations of commercial fish and shellfish like shrimp and crabs. Part of this has to do with increased demand and overfishing in the estuaries where these species breed. Scientists fear that the pollution of the salt marshes is also responsible for the decline in the species.

A number of laws have been designed to protect the plants and animals that live in these salt marshes and in other fragile wetlands habitats. The steps have helped, although the incredible life forms in these areas are not yet completely out of danger.

Tomorrow's Wetlands

How bright is the future of the Everglades and the Gulf Coast wetlands? The Everglades is the largest freshwater wetlands in the continental United States and one of the world's great biological treasures. It is home to many species of endangered or threatened plants and animals. But it is also an ecosystem in trouble. Over the past century, about half of the original Everglades has been drained, filled, and converted for farmland and other development. Much of the nutrient-filled water that once flowed naturally through the Everglades has been artificially diverted to sugarcane plantations. As a result, the entire ecosystem has suffered. Damaged wetlands cannot provide suitable habitat for the plants and animals that depend on it for survival.

In the past few decades, much has been done to prevent wetlands from being destroyed. However, the disappearance of wetlands in Florida and other Gulf Coast states remains a serious problem. We have a long way to go before many of this region's wetlands and the animals and plants that live here can be

In an effort to save the Everglades, nutrient-loving plants are introduced to the wetlands to filter out the pollution caused by the sugar cane plantations.

considered out of danger. This is why government agencies, with the help of many private environmental organizations, make saving wetlands ecosystems among their most important goals. Environmentalists believe that the uniqueness and diversity of life in wetlands warrants the highest level of protection possible.

Wetlands Laws

Many people feel that the best way to preserve wetlands is through government protection. Government agencies can best protect wetlands by establishing clear goals and policies to help pass laws that penalize people who damage and destroy wetlands. Over the last twenty-five years, significant wetlands laws have existed in the United States as part of the Clean Water Act of 1972. This important body of legislation forbids the filling, dredging, and polluting of wetlands unless permission is given by the Environmental Protection Agency (EPA), the federal agency responsible for enforcing environmental laws.

Other important laws that help protect wetlands are part of the Endangered Species Act. Passed in 1973, this law makes it illegal to hunt, trap, kill, or damage the environment of endangered and threatened species. The Endangered Species Act has saved many of the Everglades' endangered species, including the American alligator, the American crocodile, the Florida panther, the wood stork, and the manatee, from extinction due to the loss of habitat.

With these laws in place, why has the loss of wetlands continued? According to many environmentalists, part of the problem is that the laws are not properly enforced. Only a tiny fraction of the people who break the law are prosecuted, so there is little incentive to obey the laws. At the same time, many private owners of wetlands complain that the laws are too restrictive. Some private citizens don't understand why they cannot do whatever they want on their own land.

Save Our Everglades

In 1983, the state of Florida, along with several environmental groups, launched the Save Our Everglades campaign to start looking

We must study the Everglades to fully understand its complex relationships. Only then can we help to ensure its future.

at ways to preserve the troubled wetlands. The project had one clear goal: to make the Everglades look and function more like it did in 1900 than it did in 1983. Throughout the 1980s, scientists worked on this plan. However, by 1988 some interest groups in the state of Florida were still so resistant to serious environmental action that Florida was sued by the federal government for letting the sugarcane farms pollute the Everglades. A shift occurred in 1991 when the Florida state legislature passed the Everglades Forever Act, which authorized the Everglades Construction Project. Begun in 1993, the project is the largest effort ever attempted to restore an ecosystem. It will take nearly twenty years to complete and will cost hundreds of millions of dollars. Members of the task force that will head the efforts include the South Florida Water Management District, representatives of the Seminole and Miccosukee Indian tribes who live on reservations in the Everglades, and eleven federal agencies, including the U.S. Army Corps of Engineers, the Environmental Protection Agency, and the U.S. Fish and Wildlife Service. The Everglades Construction Task Force has several major undertakings planned that they hope will save the damaged ecosystem.

One of the most challenging projects in the Everglades restoration effort involves the construction of 40,000 acres (16,188 ha) of artificial marshes. These marshes will serve as a protective barrier between the sugarcane plantations and the rest of the Everglades ecosystem. The artificial wetlands are essentially huge ponds surrounded by dirt and filled with lots of nutrient-loving plants. Scientists hope that the plants will clean the water by catching and filtering out pesticides, fertilizers, and other farm runoff before it reaches the Everglades. The clean water will then be redirected back into the marsh.

Another difficult task will be to restore the Kissimmee River. Before people began tinkering with the Everglades, the Kissimmee was a 96-mile (155-km) meandering river. The river is very important to the Everglades ecosystem because it supplies most of the water to Lake Okeechobee, which lies at the northern end of the Everglades. In 1961, engineers straightened the Kissimmee River to control flooding around Lake Okeechobee and to make room for farms. Most of the water in the river was then diverted into a 52-mile (84-km) straight channel, officially named the C-38 canal.

Long before construction of the C-38 canal was completed, environmentalists predicted the ecological effects. Wetlands alongside the river that had relied on the seasonal rising and falling of water levels were drying up. As we learned earlier, this meant the loss of habitat for many forms of wildlife. Scientists expect that once the river is returned to its original path, the habitat for more than three hundred fish and wildlife species, including the endangered wood stork and snail kite, will be restored.

A total of fifty-six endangered or threatened plant and animal species live in the Everglades ecosystem. Most of these species face extinction due to habitat loss. It is estimated that habitat loss causes almost 75 percent of the extinctions now occurring. One large Everglades mammal that faces extinction due to habitat loss is the Florida panther, a type of cougar. Two hundred years ago, cougars roamed freely from Alaska to South America. These animals require a large habitat for feeding and breeding. But today, due to habitat loss, the only cougar population east of the Mississippi River is the Florida panther. Despite widespread efforts to save the panther, fewer than fifty remain in the wild. This makes the Florida panther, which lives throughout the Everglades ecosystem, one of the most endangered animals in North America.

How Do Houseplants Lose Water?

Plants are important factors in the water cycle. Through a process called transpiration, plants lose water to the atmosphere when excess water absorbed by the plant roots evaporates from the leaves. Try the following activity to find out how much water houseplants lose through transpiration.

1. Obtain several types of leafy houseplants from your home or a greenhouse. Try to get varieties that have leaves of different sizes and shapes.

2. Get several plastic sandwich bags and rubber bands.

3. Use the plastic bags to wrap up a cluster of leaves on each plant. Two to three leaves per plant should be enough. Use the rubber bands to form a tight seal around the plastic bags.

4. Water the plants and place them in a sunny spot. Wait about five days.

5. After five days, check the plastic bags. Do you see small droplets of water on the insides of the bags?

The water on the inside of the bags was released by the leaves through the process of transpiration. Which plant transpired the most water? Extend your exploration by trying different experiments. What happens if the plants are put in a windy spot? How do heat and cold affect transpiration?

The Florida panther is one of the most endangered animals in North America.

Preserving the Everglades ecosystem is the first step in saving the Florida panther. If habitat loss can be halted, biologists hope that the panther population will increase. Biologists also plan to construct more fences and pathways around major highways because automobiles pose a significant threat to the panthers. Night time speed limits have also been lowered, and panther warning signs have been installed on all major highways. A captive panther breeding program has been established. To date, ten panther kittens have been born in this program.

The Everglades and the Gulf Coast region are not yet out of danger. But because some important first steps have been taken, there is good reason to hope that these unique wetlands and the fantastic variety of wildlife within them have a future.

Glossary

adaptation a special feature or behavior developed by organisms to help them survive in a particular environment. The bulging base of the bald cypress is an adaptation that allows the tree to stand in the soft, wet soil.

algal bloom the excessive growth of algae in a pond or lake.

biodiversity the variety of plants, animals, and other living things in an area.

biological community all of the organisms that live together and interact in a particular environment.

commensalism a relationship between two organisms in which one benefits from the other (i.e., by obtaining food or protection) without harming it in any way.

decomposer an organism that gets its energy by breaking down dead organisms (i.e., by rotting them). Fungi and bacteria are decomposers that feed on dead plants and animals.

ecologist a scientist who studies the relationships among species and their environment.

ecosystem the living things in a biological community, plus the nonliving parts of the environment with which they interact.

environment all the living and nonliving things that surround an organism and affect its life.

erosion the wearing away of land by natural forces, such as wind and water.

estuary a place where freshwater mixes with the salt water of the ocean.

eutrophication the process in which bodies of water become thick with vegetation.

extinction the complete disappearance of a species from the earth.

food chain feeding relationships in which one organism is eaten by another organism, which is, in turn, eaten by a larger organism.

food web the interaction among all the food chains in a community.

habitat the place that has all the living and nonliving things that an organism needs to live and grow.

keystone species a species that has a large effect on many species in its community, or ecosystem. Alligators are considered keystone species in the Everglades ecosystem because many other species depend upon them for their survival.

mangrove swamp a coastal wetland covered with mangroves, trees that grow on salty, muddy shores with their bases submerged in water.

marsh a type of wetland characterized by the growth of nonwoody plants such as grasses. The Everglades is a marsh.

mud flat low-lying muddy land that is covered with water during high tide and exposed during low tide.

organism a living thing, such as a plant or animal.

photosynthesis the process by which plants and some other organisms that have chlorophyll use light, carbon dioxide, and water to make sugars and other substances.

precipitation water that falls to Earth from the atmosphere in the form of rain, hail, sleet, or snow.

predator an animal that hunts or kills other animals for food, i.e., snakes, alligators, and eagles.

primary consumer an animal that eats plants, i.e., muskrats, squirrels, and birds.

producer an organism (generally a plant) that converts solar energy to chemical energy by photosynthesis.

runoff water that is not absorbed by land and flows across Earth's surface into rivers and streams.

salt marsh a coastal wetland covered with grasses and grasslike plants.

species a group of organisms that closely resemble each other and can interbreed with one another in nature.

swamp a type of wetland where many hardwood trees and shrubs grow.

water cycle the process by which water is transformed from vapor in the atmosphere to precipitation on land and water surfaces and ultimately back into the air.

wetland an area of land that is covered with water for all or part of the year.

Further Exploration

Books

Bryant, Jennifer. *Marjory Stoneman Douglas: Voice of the Everglades.* Earth Keeper Series. New York: Twenty-First Century Books, 1992.

Caitlin, Stephen. *Wonders of Swamps and Marshes.* Mahwah, NJ: Troll Associates, 1993.

Lavies, Bianca. *Mangrove Wilderness: Nature's Nursery.* New York: Dutton Press, 1994.

Greenaway, Theresa. *Swamp Life.* Look Closer Series. New York: Dorling Kindersley, 1993.

Organizations

Coastal Conservation Association
4801 Woodway, Suite 220 W
Houston, TX 77056
(713) 626-4222

Florida Audubon Society
1331 Palmetto Avenue, Suite 110
Winter Park, FL 32789
(407) 539-5700

Friends of the Everglades
101 Westward Drive, #2
Miami Springs, FL 33166
(305) 669-0858

National Audubon Society
700 Broadway
New York, NY 10003
(212) 979-3000

National Wildlife Federation
1400 16th Street, NW
Washington, DC 20036-2266
(202) 797-6800

The Nature Conservancy
1815 N. Lynn Street
Arlington, VA 22209
(703) 841-5300

Index

Page numbers for illustrations are in **boldface**.